WAY SE 4/05

DO NOT REMOVE
CARDS FROM POCKET

■ Science Experiments for Young People ■

Environmental Experiments

About

LAND

Thomas R. Rybolt

and

Robert C. Mebane

ENSLOW PUBLISHERS, INC.
Bloy St. and Ramsey Ave.   P.O. Box 38
Box 777   Aldershot
Hillside, N.J. 07205   Hants GU12 6BP
U.S.A.   U.K.

For my son, Ben, with love — TR

For my Aunt Forney and to the memory
of her husband, Rock — RM

Acknowledgements
We wish to thank Robert Tate, Richard Pekala, Clarence
Murphy, Mickey Sarquis, and Ron Perkins for reading and
making helpful comments on the manuscript.

Copyright © 1993 by Thomas R. Rybolt and Robert C. Mebane

Library of Congress Cataloging-in-Publication Data

Rybolt, Thomas R.
  Environmental experiments about land / Thomas R. Rybolt and Robert
  C. Mebane.
       p. cm. — (Science experiments for young people)
  Includes index.
    Summary: Presents experiments that explore the properties and
  erosion of soil, recycling, and organic waste.
    ISBN 0-89490-411-6
    1. Soils–Experiments–Juvenile literature. 2. Soil erosion–
  Experiments–Juvenile literature. 3. Recycling (Waste, etc.)–
  Experiments–Juvenile literature. 4. Organic wastes–Experiments–
  Juvenile literature. [1. Soils–Experiments. 2. Recycling
  (Waste)–Experiments. 3. Refuse and refuse disposal–Experiments.
  4. Experiments.] I. Mebane, Robert C. II. Title. III. Series:
  Rybolt, Thomas R. Science experiments for young people.
  S593.R92 1993
  631.4'078–dc20   93-15581
                                                          CIP
                                                          AC

Printed in the United States of America

10 9 8 7 6 5 4 3 2 1

Illustration Credit: Kimberly Austin

Cover Illustration: ©Manfred Gottschalk/Tom Stack & Associates

CONTENTS

series contents for
SCIENCE EXPERIMENTS
FOR YOUNG PEOPLE

Introduction

Earth

Earth, our home in space, has supported life for billions of years. But with a growing human population, people are having a greater effect on the environment than ever before. Together we must learn about the problems facing our environment and work to protect the earth.

There are many ways we can work together to protect the earth. We can ask adults to use more fuel-efficient cars (cars that get more miles per gallon of gasoline). We can ride bikes or walk instead of getting rides in cars. We can recycle aluminum, paper, plastic, and glass, and we can plant trees. We can save energy by turning off lights when they are not in use. We can save energy by not keeping rooms and buildings too hot in the winter or too cold in the summer. Another way we can help the earth is to learn more about the environment.

This series of environmental books is designed to help you better understand our environment by doing experiments with air, water, land, and life. Each book is divided into chapters on topics of environmental concern or importance. There is a brief introduction to each chapter followed by a group of experiments related to the chapter topic. This series of environmental experiment books is intended to be used and not just read. It is your guide to doing, observing, and thinking about your environment.

By understanding our environment, we can learn to protect the earth and to use our natural resources wisely for generations to come.

Atoms and Molecules

Understanding something about atoms and molecules will help you understand our environment. Everything in the world around us is made of atoms and molecules. Atoms are the basic building blocks of all things. There are about 100 different kinds of atoms. Molecules are combinations of tightly bound atoms. For example, a water molecule is a combination of two hydrogen atoms and one oxygen atom.

Molecules that are made of only a few atoms are very small. Just one drop of water contains about two million quadrillion (2,000,000,000,000,000,000,000) water molecules.

Polymers are large molecules that may contain millions of atoms. Important natural polymers include natural rubber, starch, and DNA. Some important artificial polymers are nylon, which is used in making fabrics, polyethylene, which is used in making plastic bags and plastic bottles, and polystyrene, which is used in making styrofoam cups and insulation.

Atoms are made of smaller particles called electrons, protons, and neutrons. The nucleus is the center of the atom and contains protons and neutrons. Protons are positively charged, and neutrons have no charge. Electrons are negatively charged and surround the nucleus and give the atom its size.

Atoms and molecules that are charged are called ions. Ions have either a positive charge or a negative charge. Positive ions have more protons than electrons. Negative ions have more electrons than protons. Sodium chloride, which is the chemical name for table salt, is made of positive sodium ions and negative chlorine ions.

Atoms, ions, and molecules can combine in chemical reactions to make new substances. Chemical reactions can change one substance into another or break one substance down into smaller parts made of molecules, atoms, or ions.

Science and Experiments

One way to learn more about the environment and science is to do experiments. Science experiments provide a way of asking questions and finding answers. The results that come from experiments and observations increase our knowledge and improve our understanding of the world around us.

Science will never have all the answers because there

are always new questions to ask. However science is the most important way we gather new knowledge about our world.

This series of environmental experiment books is a collection of experiments that you can do at home or at school. As you read about science and do experiments, you will learn more about our planet and its environment.

Not every experiment you do will work the way you expect every time. Something may be different in the experiment when you do it. Repeat the experiment if it gives an unexpected result and think about what may be different.

Not all of the experiments in this book give immediate results. Some experiments in this book will take time to see observable results. Some of the experiments in this book may take a shorter time than that suggested in the experiment. Some experiments may take a longer time than suggested.

Each experiment is divided into five parts: (1) materials, (2) procedure, (3) observations, (4) discussion, and (5) other things to try. The materials are what you need to do the experiment. The procedure is what you do. The observations are what you see. The discussion explains what your observations tell you about the environment. The other things to try are additional questions and experiments.

Safety Note

Make Sure You:

- Obtain an adult's permission before you do these experiments and activities.
- Get an adult to watch you when you do an experiment. They enjoy seeing experiments too.
- Follow the specific directions given for each experiment.
- Clean up after each experiment.

Note to Teachers, Parents, and Other Adults

Science is not merely a collection of facts but a way of thinking. As a teacher, parent, or adult friend, you can play a key role in maintaining and encouraging a young person's interest in science and the surrounding world. As you do environmental experiments with a young person, you may find your own curiosity being expanded. Experiments are one way to learn more about the air, water, land, and life upon which we all depend.

I. Introduction to Soil

Soil is the fine, loose surface material covering the earth. Although sometimes taken for granted, soil plays many crucial roles in our environment. Without soil, it would be hard to imagine having life on earth. Soil is the link between the living and nonliving worlds.

Most of the food of the world is grown in soil. Soil supports these growing plants and serves as a reservoir of water, air, and nutrients that are essential to living plants.

Soil is a complex material that can differ from one location to another. Soil that is hard consists mostly of clay and sand particles. In addition to these mineral particles, soil contains water, air, and decaying plant and animal matter. Also found in most soils are microorganisms, such as bacteria and fungi, and soil animals, such as earthworms. Soil microorganisms and animals are nature's recyclers. They break down and change dead plant and animal matter into nutrients to support living plants. In turn, the plants serve as food.

Unfortunately, those factors that make soil essential to life also make soil easy to contaminate and pollute. It is important that we take care of the soil so that the soil can take care of us and other life on earth. In the following experiments, you will learn more about what soil is, and what it looks like.

Experiment #1

Is Soil Made of One Layer or Several Layers?

Materials

A shovel   A grassy area

A magnifying glass   Ruler

Several sheets of newspaper

Procedure

ASK AN ADULT TO HELP YOU CHOOSE A GRASSY AREA WHERE YOU CAN DIG A HOLE ABOUT TWO FEET DEEP. Also, you may need the adult's help in digging the hole.

Spread several sheets of newspaper, one on top of the other, next to the grassy spot where you are going to dig your hole. Carefully dig up the grass in large clumps and set the clumps of grass next to the sheets of newspaper. You will need to remove the grass from an area about the size of a circle two feet across. (When this activity is completed, you will fill in the hole and replace the clumps of grass.)

Once the grass is removed, dig a hole about two feet deep. Place the soil you remove on the layer of newspapers. Try to make the wall of the hole straight up and down as you dig.

Starting at the top and moving down to the bottom of your hole, look carefully at the soil along the wall of your hole. You can use a magnifying glass to look at the soil along the wall of your hole. Rub some soil from the various layers between your fingers.

After you have made your observations, fill in your hole with the soil that is on the newspapers. Make sure to replace the clumps of grass on the top of the filled-in hole.

Observations

Do you see various layers of soil along the wall of the hole? Do the layers of soil have different colors? What colors are the layers of soil?

What color is the soil on the bottom of the clumps of grass? Do you see dead grass and other debris on the top surface of the clumps of grass?

Does soil from the various layers feel the same or different? Does some of the soil feel gritty and some feel slippery? Do you see rocks in your soil? Are there more rocks at the bottom of your hole than at the top?

Do you see any earthworms, beetles, or other burrowing animals in the various layers of soil?

Discussion

Depending on where you live, your results may be different than what is discussed here.

Soil usually forms in a series of horizontal layers. Together, these layers of soil are called the soil profile. Topsoil, subsoil, and loose bedrock are the names given to the layers that make up the soil profile.

As the name suggests, topsoil is the top layer of soil. The topsoil layer is usually dark in color and may even be the darkest layer in a soil profile. The depth of the topsoil layer usually ranges from under an inch (under 2.54 centimeters) to over a foot (over 30.5 centimeters).

Topsoil contains tiny mineral particles like sand, silt, and clay and dead and decaying plant and animal material.

This dead and decaying plant and animal material is called humus. Humus is important to living plants and animals because it is an important source of nutrients. Creatures that live in the soil, like earthworms, insects, millipedes, centipedes, and snails, live mostly in the topsoil because the topsoil is rich in nutrients. These living creatures help keep the topsoil rich in nutrients by helping in the breakdown of dead plant and animal material. A sample of rich topsoil about the size of your thumb may contain millions of bacteria and other microorganisms that help break down dead plant and animal material.

Under the topsoil is the subsoil. Subsoil is usually a lighter color than topsoil. This is because the subsoil contains less humus. Since subsoil contains less humus, fewer living creatures are found in this layer. The subsoil layer is usually thicker than the topsoil layer. It normally ranges in width from several inches to several feet.

The subsoil layer usually contains more silt and clay particles than sand particles. Clay particles are much finer than sand particles. Soil that contains mostly clay feels slippery. Soil that contains mostly sand feels gritty.

Topsoil is usually more loose than subsoil. Subsoil that contains mostly clay can be tightly packed. Only the roots of large plants, like trees and some bushes, can penetrate packed subsoil. The roots of small plants like grass and flowers are found only in topsoil because they are not strong enough to penetrate the subsoil.

Below the subsoil is loose bedrock. You may not be able to see loose bedrock in your hole because your subsoil layer may be too thick. Loose bedrock consists of coarsely broken rocks. These coarse rocks were once part of a large piece of rock called bedrock. Bedrock is the parent material of soil. If you travel on a road that has been cut through a mountain, it is usually possible to see bedrock.

Other Things to Try

Ask an adult to help you repeat this activity in a wooded area. Do you get similar results? Is the topsoil layer deeper in a wooded area? The dead tree leaves and twigs found on the surface in a wooded area are called litter. Litter is a major source of humus in a wooded area. The litter in a grassy area would be dead grass. There is usually more litter in a forest. This means the topsoil may be deeper in a forest than in a grassy area.

Have you ever traveled on a road that was cut through a hill or mountain? If you have, you may have noticed a more complete exposed soil profile, including the underlying bedrock.

Experiment #2

Can Different Sizes of Soil Particles Be Easily Separated?

Materials

Soil   Water

A large jar with a tight-fitting lid

Procedure

Add soil to a large jar until the jar is about one-third full. Now fill the jar nearly full with water. Tighten the lid on the jar and shake the jar for fifteen seconds. Set the jar in a spot where it will not be disturbed. Allow the soil in the jar to settle overnight. The next day look at the layers in the jar.

After you have finished with the experiment, ask an adult to show you a place outside where you can dump the soil that is in the jar. Do not dump the soil in a sink because it may clog the sink drain. Rinse the jar several times with water. Make sure to pour the rinse water outside on the ground and not in a sink.

Observations

What color is the soil you placed in the jar? What color does the water in the jar become when you shake the jar? Does any of the soil settle immediately to the bottom of the jar when you stop shaking?

How many layers of solid material form in the jar after the jar sits overnight? What color are the layers? Do the particles in the bottom layer appear larger than particles in the other layers? Which of the layers appears the thickest?

What color is the water that is above the layers of soil? Is there any material floating on the surface of the water?

Discussion

Depending on the type of soil in your area, your results may be different than what is discussed here. If your results are significantly different, then repeat this experiment with potting soil or topsoil that you can purchase at hardware stores, garden stores, and large grocery stores.

Soils are classified by their texture and by the size of the mineral particles in the soil. Soil texture is a measure of the amounts of sand, silt, and clay present in a soil sample. Sand, silt, and clay are names used to classify the size of particles found in soil.

The largest soil particles are sand and the smallest are clay. Soil particles between sand and clay are silt.

Sand, silt, and clay particles in soil can be separated by the method used in this experiment, which is called settling. When you shake soil containing sand, silt, and clay in a jar with a large amount of water, the individual soil particles become separated from each other. The soil particles also become suspended in the water. When you stop shaking the jar, small rocks and the larger sand particles settle to the bottom of the jar first. They settle to the bottom first because they are heavier (more dense). After most of the sand has settled, silt particles start to settle out of the water. Clay particles, which are the smallest and lightest soil particles, settle out last.

If the soil you use for this experiment contains sand, silt, and clay, then you will see three separate layers. The bottom layer will consist mainly of sand. The middle layer will be silt, and the top layer will be clay. The clay layer will probably be lighter in color because the sand and silt layers may contain humus particles, which are dark in color. Humus is organic material made from the decay of plants and animals. Humus becomes heavy when it absorbs water. This is why humus settles out with the sand and silt particles. You may also see material floating on top of the water. This material is probably pieces of leaves, twigs, and other plant material.

By looking at how thick the layers are in your jar, you can learn something about the texture of your soil. If the thickest layer in your jar is sand, then the texture of your soil is sandy. If the thickest layer in your jar is clay, then the texture of your soil is clay.

An ideal soil texture is called loam. Loam is soil that contains equal amounts of sand and silt, and some clay. Loam is ideal for plants because it holds well nutrients, water, and air.

Other Things to Try

Ask an adult to help you collect different soil samples near where you live. Repeat this experiment with the soil samples that were collected. Do you get similar results with different soil samples?

Repeat this experiment with potting soil. How do your results with potting soil compare with soils taken from the ground?

II. Properties of Soil

Although soil is a complex mixture of different materials, all soils are made up of mineral particles and organic matter. The mineral particles of soil are sand and clay. The organic matter in the soil is called humus and comes from animal waste and the decomposition or breakdown of dead plants and animals.

The amounts of clay, sand, and humus in a soil determine the soil type. Different soil types can have different soil properties. Some important soil properties include: How much air and water can the soil hold? How fast does water move through the soil? Does the soil change because of acid or base? In the experiments that follow, you will find answers to these questions, and you will learn more about different soils and soil properties.

Experiment #3

What Are Clay and Sand and How Do They Differ?

Materials

Sand	Water
A magnifying glass	

Artist or modeling clay (available in art, craft, and toy stores)

Procedure

Wet your hands and constantly squeeze a piece of clay about the size of your thumb for thirty seconds to soften the clay. Now, rub a piece of this softened clay between the thumb and index finger of one hand. Describe how the clay feels.

Wet your fingers and rub some sand between the thumb and index finger of one hand. Describe how the sand feels.

Study the clay and sand under a magnifying glass and describe what you see.

Observations

Does the modeling clay feel slippery or rough when you rub it between your thumb and finger? Does the sand feel slippery or rough when you rub it between your thumb and finger?

Are the particles that make up the clay smaller than the particles of sand? What shapes do you see in the grains of sand? Are some of the grains of sand round?

Discussion

The modeling clay should feel slippery when you rub a piece of it between your fingers. In contrast, the sand should feel rough and gritty.

You should also notice that it is easy to see individual

grains of sand. However, even with a magnifying glass, it is difficult to see individual particles in a piece of clay. This is because clay particles are so small. Clay particles are much smaller than grains of sand.

Clay and sand are the major mineral solids found in soil. Clay and sand are made by the natural breakdown of minerals and rocks. Clay comes mainly from the mineral feldspar. Sand comes mainly from rock such as granite that contains quartz.

Both clay and sand contain silica. Silica is a chemical substance made of atoms of silicon and oxygen.

Sand is mostly silica because sand comes from quartz, which is nearly pure silica. Glass, like that used to make windows and glass containers, is another type of silica.

Clay is silica that also contains aluminum atoms and water. In addition to aluminum atoms, other metal atoms can be found in clay. These other metals can make clay colored. For example, red clay contains iron atoms.

Clay particles are extremely small with diameters of 0.002 millimeters and smaller. (It takes about 25 millimeters to equal 1 inch.) In contrast, grains of sand range in size from 0.062 to 2.0 millimeters. An average size grain of sand is about five hundred times bigger than the largest clay particle.

Geologists use the term silt to describe soil particles that are larger than clay particles but smaller than sand. The diameter of silt particles is between 0.002 and 0.062 millimeters. Silt particles can be either mostly silica, like sand, or can contain the same chemical substances found in clay.

If you could see clay particles, they would look like tiny thin plates. These thin plates of clay easily slide over one another when clay is wet. This is why clay feels slippery when it is wet. However, the clay plates stick together when they are dry.

Grains of sand can have many different shapes. The shapes of grains of sand can tell you if the sand has been in moving water for a long time. If the grains of sand appear round or have smooth corners, they have been carried by water. Grains of sand that have sharp edges have not been carried by water.

Other Things to Try

The next time you are near a body of moving water, like a creek or river, ask an adult to help you collect some sand from the bank bordering the water. NEVER GO NEAR THE EDGE OF A BODY OF WATER WITHOUT AN ADULT. Do the grains of sand have a round shape? Can you explain why?

Clay is used to make ceramic objects such as bowls, plates, and flower pots. The clay is first shaped while it is wet. Next, the soft clay object is placed in an oven to drive off the water. This causes the thin plates of clay to lock together, forming a hard material. To show that clay can be made hard, rub the outside of an unglazed, clay flower pot. Describe how the surface feels.

Experiment #4

Does Sand or Soil Hold More Water?

Materials

Potting soil	Sand
Water	Two coffee filters
Measuring cups	Two aluminum pie pans
Two clear plastic cups	A sharpened pencil
Tape	A felt pen
Two medium-sized paper cups	

Procedure

You need to use dry potting soil and dry sand for this experiment. To dry these materials, spread several handfuls of potting soil in one of the pie pans and several handfuls of sand in the other pie pan. Place both pans in the sun on a warm day and leave them in the sun for several hours.

Place a piece of tape on each paper cup and each plastic cup. Label one paper cup and one plastic cup "soil" and the other paper cup and plastic cup "sand." Use the sharpened end of a pencil to punch four holes slightly larger than the size of the pencil lead into the bottom of each paper cup. Place a coffee filter in each paper cup. Use your fingers to push the coffee filters into the paper cups. The paper cups should be lined with the coffee filters.

Loosely pack the paper cup labeled "soil" three-fourths full with dry potting soil. Fill the paper cup labeled "sand" three-fourths full with the dry sand.

While holding the paper cup containing the potting soil over the plastic cup labeled "soil," slowly pour one cup of water over the potting soil. Make sure to collect the water coming from the bottom of the paper cup into the plastic cup labeled "soil." Use a measuring cup to measure the amount of water that collects in the plastic cup labeled "soil" when no more water drips from the paper cup.

While holding the paper cup containing the sand over the plastic cup labeled "sand," slowly pour one cup of water over the sand. Make sure to collect the water coming from the bottom of the paper cup into the plastic cup labeled "sand." Use a measuring cup to measure the amount of water that collects in the plastic cup labeled "sand" when no more water drips from the paper cup.

Ask an adult to show you a place outside where you can dump the potting soil and sand on the ground. Do not dump them in a sink because they may clog the sink drain.

Observations

Describe the appearance of the potting soil and the sand before and after the water has been added to each. How are they different?

How much water did you collect in the plastic cup labeled "soil?" How much water did you collect in the plastic cup labeled "sand?" Does more water pass through the potting soil or the sand? Which material holds more water?

Discussion

Water soaks into the ground because there are tiny openings between the particles that make up the soil in

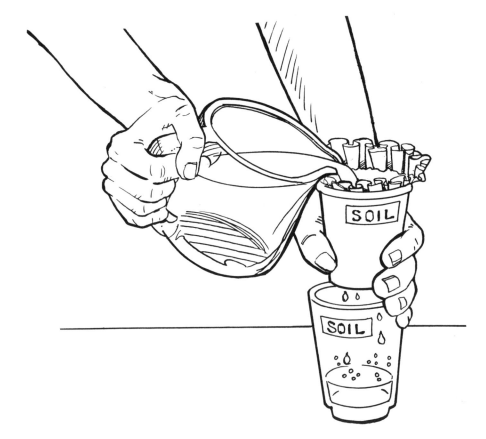

the ground. These tiny openings are called pore spaces and are similar to the openings in a sponge.

Porosity is the measure of the amount of pore spaces in a soil. A soil with a high porosity has more pore spaces than a soil with a low porosity. A soil can be made less porous by tightly packing together the particles that make up the soil.

Pore spaces in the soil contain mostly air when the soil is dry. When water soaks into the ground, the water pushes out the air and fills in the pore spaces in the soil.

Water that enters into the pore spaces in the soil can either be trapped in the pore spaces or can pass through the pore spaces and move to other parts of the soil. If water passes easily through the pore spaces, the soil is said to be permeable. Permeability is a measure of how easily water passes through soil. Soil that holds water helps plants grow. Water is essential for a plant to live and grow.

The amount of water a soil can hold depends on the soil's porosity and permeability. Soil that is porous and has a low permeability will easily hold water.

In this experiment, you should find that less water passes through the cup containing the potting soil than the cup containing the sand. This means that potting soil holds more water than sand.

Sand contains many pore spaces because the individual grains of sand do not pack tightly together. Sand is porous, but sand does not readily hold water because it is quite permeable. Water moves easily through the pore spaces in the sand. This is why you should have collected more water in the plastic cup labeled "sand" than in the cup labeled "soil."

Soils that are rich in humus can hold large amounts of water. Humus is organic material from the decay of dead plants and animals. Like a sponge, humus swells as it quickly absorbs water. Many gardeners add compost, which is humus made from yard and vegetable waste, to their garden soil to increase the water-holding properties of their soil.

Other Things to Try

Although soil that is mostly clay may be porous, water passes through it very slowly. This means clay has a low permeability. To show that clay has a low permeability, pour some water on a flattened piece of modeling clay in an aluminum pie pan. Does the water pass through the clay or does it bead up on the clay?

Ask an adult to help you collect different soil samples around where you live. Repeat this experiment with the soil samples that were collected. Do the different soil samples hold different amounts of water?

Experiment #5

How Can You Determine the Acidity or Alkalinity of Soil-like Material?

Materials

Red cabbage leaves	Measuring spoons
A large jar with lid	A measuring cup
A permanent marker	Hot water
White sand	Vinegar
Three spoons	Water
A large bowl	

Pickling lime (available in grocery stores)

Three small glass jars (baby-food size)

Procedure

ASK AN ADULT TO HELP YOU WITH THIS EXPERIMENT. DO NOT GET ANY OF THE PICKLING LIME ON YOUR SKIN OR IN YOUR EYES. PICKLING LIME CAN HARM YOUR EYES AND IRRITATE YOUR SKIN.

Tear pieces of red cabbage into small pieces about the size of your thumb. Fill a large bowl with pieces of red cabbage. Cover the pieces of cabbage with hot water from a sink faucet or water heated on a stove. Wait about twenty minutes until the water turns purple. Pour the purple water into a large jar for use in this experiment. For future experiments, save extra cabbage juice in a closed jar in a refrigerator.

Use a permanent marker to label the three small jars "1", "2," and "3." Add one-eighth cup of white sand to each of these jars.

Add one-eighth teaspoon of pickling line and one-fourth teaspoon of water to the jar labeled "1." Stir with a clean spoon for about twenty seconds until the water, lime, and sand are mixed together. Use a clean spoon to add one-fourth teaspoon of water to the jar labeled "2." Stir the water into the sand. To the jar labeled "3," add one-fourth teaspoon of vinegar. Again, stir this mixture of vinegar and sand with a clean spoon until well mixed. You now have three jars that simulate different types of acidity or alkalinity of soil.

Add two teaspoons of purple cabbage juice to the first jar and stir with a clean spoon. Add two teaspoons of purple cabbage juice to the second jar and stir with a clean spoon. Add two teaspoons of purple cabbage juice to the third jar and stir with a clean spoon.

Observations

What color is the sand in each jar before the cabbage juice is added? Does the sand in the three jars look the same? What color is the sand in each jar after the cabbage juice is added?

Discussion

Sand is not the same as soil. This experiment was done using sand to simulate or take the place of true soil because the color changes are easier to see. Soil is a complicated mixture of particles of sand, silt, and clay. Soil also contains air, water, and decayed plant and animal matter called humus. The decomposition or breakdown of dead plants forms different types of humic acids. Soil is a mixture of different compounds,

including humic acids, that cause soil to be acidic, neutral, or alkaline.

The sand in each of the jars should look identical before cabbage juice is added. However, once the cabbage juice is added, the first jar's sand should turn green, the second jar's sand should turn purple, and the third jar's sand should turn red.

In this experiment, the sand in the first jar turned green because lime made the soil alkaline. The sand in the second jar remained purple because it was neutral. The sand in the third jar turned red because the acetic acid in vinegar made this sand acidic. Pure sand is neutral.

Cabbage juice contains molecules called indicators that change color depending on the amount of acidity or alkalinity. In very acidic conditions, cabbage juice is red. In very alkaline conditions, cabbage juice is green. In slightly acidic to neutral conditions, cabbage juice is purple. In neutral to slightly alkaline conditions, cabbage juice is blue. When something is not acid or alkaline, it is neutral.

Most vegetables grow best in slightly acidic to neutral soil. However, crops such as soybeans and alfalfa grow best in more alkaline soil.

Too much alkalinity in soil can cause yellowing of leaves and decrease plant growth. Too much acidity in soil can cause aluminum ions or compounds present in soil to be released and absorbed by plants where it acts like a poison and kills the plants. The extra acid can also change the soil so roots cannot absorb important nutrients from the soil. Also, earthworms that feed on decaying plants and release important nutrients into soil are less active if the soil becomes too acidic.

Excess acidity in soil can come from acid rain. Normal rain water is slightly acidic because carbon dioxide in the air dissolves in water. However, in some parts of the world, there is more acid in the rain than normal. This type of rain is called acid rain. Acid rain is caused by nitrogen oxides and sulfur dioxide pollutants.

Other Things to Try

Put together two or three coffee filters and fill them with about a cup of soil. Pour enough red cabbage water through this soil until it drips out of the bottom. Collect the water that drips out of the bottom of the coffee filter. Does the water change color? Repeat this procedure with fresh soil samples in clean coffee filters using the purple, blue, or green cabbage water. Then try adding one-fourth teaspoon of lime to one cup samples of soil and repeating this testing. Does the water change color?

Try testing different samples of soil to determine the acidity or alkalinity of the soil. You may want to obtain a simple soil acidity test kit from a nursery and plant store or pH paper from an aquarium/pet store to more exactly determine the pH.

III. Land Changes and Erosion

The gradual wearing down of rocks by wind, water, and ice creates small particles of soil. This process of making small particles from larger objects is a type of erosion called weathering. We depend on these small particles of sand, silt, and clay to make soil and to grow food.

Land plants use their roots to obtain water and nutrients from the soil. Plants not only depend on soil, but they also help make more soil. Roots and growing plants can help break apart rocks and larger particles.

Although erosion is an important source of small particles from which soil is made, erosion can also destroy soil. Soil erosion is the unwanted movement of soil from one place to another because of moving water or air. Moving air and water can carry away the nutrient-rich outer layer of topsoil.

Soil quality can be damaged by irrigation practices that cause salt to build up in the soil. Improper farming practices can also damage soil quality.

In these experiments, you will learn how soil is lost from wind and rain, how salt can become concentrated in irrigated soil, and how growing lichens help change rocks to soil.

Experiment #6

Can Moving Air Cause
Erosion of Uncovered Soil?

Materials

Two aluminum pie pans   Two pieces of newspaper

A patch of growing grass   A balloon

A trowel or small shovel

Procedure

Have an adult help you use a trowel or shovel to dig up a small patch of grass (about the size of your fist) including the roots and attached soil. Use the trowel to collect about a cupful of loose soil from where the patch of grass was removed. You will need to collect this sample when the ground is dry. Make sure the loose soil you collect is not wet.

Spread out two pieces of newspaper on the ground. Place an aluminum pie pan in the center of each piece of newspaper. Sprinkle the loose soil into the first pie pan and set the patch of grass in the second pie pan.

Blow up the balloon as full as you can and pinch the opening of the balloon so the air does not escape. Hold the balloon about eight inches above the center of the pan filled with loose soil. Release the opening of the balloon but hold the balloon in place so the air from the balloon blows directly on the center of the pan of soil. Repeat this procedure with the balloon, but this time let the air from the balloon blow directly on top of the patch of grass in the second pie pan.

After you have finished making your observations, you can return the loose soil and patch of grass to the ground from where they were removed. The grass should continue to grow.

Observations

Did air from the balloon blow soil out of the first pan onto the newspaper? Did air from the balloon blow soil, from the patch of grass, out of the second pan onto the newspaper? Was there a difference in the movement of soil from the first and second pans?

Discussion

You probably found that much more soil was blown out of the pan filled with loose dirt than the pan containing the patch of grass. The air escaping from the balloon acts like the wind that blows across the surface of the earth. This moving air can cause soil to be moved from one place to another.

Much of the land area of the earth is covered with soil. Average soil contains air, water, and a mixture of small particles of sand, silt, and clay. Soil also contains an organic material called humus. (Humus is the brown or black material in soil that comes from the decay of plant and animal matter. Humus is the part of the soil that helps provide nutrients for plants to grow.) The outermost surface layer of soil is called topsoil. Topsoil is richer in important nutrients and darker than the subsoil beneath it.

Unfortunately, each year the farmers of the world must try to feed millions more people with billions of tons (one ton is 2,000 pounds) less topsoil. Essential topsoil is being lost because of the erosion of soil. Soil

erosion is the unwanted movement of soil from one place to another because of moving water or air.

In the 1930s, there were huge dust storms in the midwestern United States. These storms were caused by dry weather and poor farming practices. Huge amounts of soil were blown away as dry dust. The soil in states such as Kansas, Colorado, Oklahoma, and New Mexico was damaged. Many people left their family farms. Although the land has recovered enough to grow crops today, it reminds us of the importance of protecting our soil.

Around the world today, soil erosion is being caused by poor land management practices. Overgrazing by livestock and deforestation also contribute to soil erosion. (Deforestation is removal of trees from the land.) Allowing livestock such as cattle and sheep to overgraze (eat too much vegetation in one area) can cause plant cover to be removed and expose topsoil to erosion. From this experiment, it is clear that the cover of plants on the soil and the roots from plants can keep soil from being blown away. One method used by farmers to prevent wind erosion is windbreaks—thick rows of trees and plants that line fields. A windbreak can cut wind speeds in half and thus help prevent erosion when fields are bare.

Other Things to Try

Repeat this experiment using sand (found on beaches and in sandboxes). Does the sand blow out of the pie pan? Now fill the pie pan with sand and add enough to water to wet the sand. Blow up the balloon and let the air blow on this wet sand. Is the wet sand blown out of the pie pan as much as the dry sand? Keeping soil moist helps prevent wind erosion.

Try repeating this experiment with dry sand but move the balloon farther away. Try to determine the minimum wind from the balloon that will blow sand out of the pie pan.

Try mixing sand and gravel and repeating this experiment. You should find that the smaller sand will be blown out while the larger pieces of gravel remain.

Experiment #7

Can Moving Water Cause Erosion of Uncovered Soil?

Materials

Two aluminum pie pans   A measuring cup

A patch of growing grass   Water

A trowel or small shovel

Procedure

Have an adult help you use a trowel or shovel to dig up a small patch of grass (about the size of your fist). Make sure you include the roots and attached soil. Some loose dirt may fall off the roots. Use the trowel to collect about a cupful of soil from where the patch of grass was removed. You will need to collect this sample when the ground is dry. Make sure the loose soil you collect is not wet.

Make a pile of soil about the size of your fist in the middle of the first pie pan. Set the patch of grass in the middle of the second pie pan.

Fill the measuring cup with one-half cup of water. Hold the measuring cup about one foot (30 centimeters) above the pile of loose soil. Slowly pour the water directly on the center of the pan of soil. Continue pouring all the water on the soil. Fill the measuring cup with one-half cup of water again. Repeat the pouring procedure but this time pour the water directly on top of the patch of grass in the second pie pan.

After you have finished making your observations, you can return the soil and patch of grass to the ground from where they were removed. The grass should continue to grow.

Observations

Did the falling water cause the soil to spread out into the first pan? Did the falling water cause soil from the

clump of grass to spread out into the second pan? Was there a difference in the movement of soil in the first and second pans?

Discussion

You probably found that much more soil was spread out into the pan filled with a pile of dirt than the one containing a patch of grass. Moving water can cause erosion, or the movement of particles of soil from one place to another. Covering the surface of the soil with plants is very important to prevent erosion and loss of topsoil.

Weathering is the natural process of wearing down larger rocks and pebbles to form small mineral particles. These particles include sand, silt, and clay, which are the mineral portion of soil. Soil also contains an organic portion called humus, which comes from the decay of living matter.

Weathering is a slow process that can gradually build up soil. Wind, flowing water, and slowly moving glaciers all contribute to the breakdown of large rocks and the formation of small particles of sand, silt, and clay.

When water trapped in the cracks of rocks freezes, it expands and can cause rocks to break into smaller pieces. Wind can carry dust particles and wear down surfaces. Moving water can carry small particles that scrape surfaces. The dramatic effects of moving water are seen in the places like the Grand Canyon where erosion from the Colorado River has cut a huge gorge, or opening, in the ground. Glaciers can slowly move across the surface of the land and carry rocks that scrape the surface. When ice ages end and glaciers grow smaller, the melting glaciers leave smaller particles behind.

The gradual production of soil is a benefit for supporting plant life, but rain and rapidly moving water can wash away nutrient-filled topsoil necessary for growing crops. In many areas around the world where people have cleared forests on hills to have more land for growing crops, the benefit has not lasted long. The cleared hills lack the necessary cover to prevent erosion from rainwater flowing down the hills. The valuable topsoil is washed down the hills into streams and carried in rivers toward the sea. More and more, people are recognizing the importance of understanding and working with nature rather than against nature.

There are a variety of methods farmers use to reduce the erosion of valuable topsoil. These methods include contour plowing, strip cropping, cover crops, conservation tillage, terracing, and windbreaks.

In contour plowing, a farmer follows the natural slopes of the land rather than plowing straight up or down hills. This practice prevents runoff of soil after a heavy rain. In strip cropping, thick-growing crops are alternated with other crops to prevent erosion on sloping land. The use of cover crops like grass and alfalfa on fields not in active use keeps the soil covered. In conservation tillage, the remains from the previous crop are left on the surface to protect the soil rather than being plowed under.

Terracing the land prevents soil from being washed down steep slopes. Flat terraces are made on the side of a hill so it looks more like a series of steps than a hill. Rice terraces have been used for thousands of years in mountainous regions of Asia. Windbreaks are thick rows of trees and plants that line fields and reduce wind speeds.

Other Things to Try

Repeat this experiment for covered and uncovered soil with the pie pan tipped at an angle rather than being flat. Does the soil wash away more rapidly when the pan is flat or tilted? As the slope, or angle, of the pie pan is made greater, does the erosion become worse?

Look at the bottom of the clump of grass. Do you see the roots that extend throughout the soil? Can you explain why these roots help hold the soil together?

Look for places in your community where you can find examples of water erosion. Can you identify the reasons why erosion is occurring at these places?

Experiment #8

Can Rocks Be Broken Down by Plants?

Materials

Small screwdriver   A magnifying glass

A rock with lichens on its surface

Procedure

Find a rock with lichens on its surface. Lichens usually appear as grayish-green or yellow patches on rocks. Depending on where you live, lichens may or may not be common on rocks.

Examine the lichens with a magnifying glass. Use a small screwdriver to carefully scrape off a piece of lichen about the size of a small pea from the surface of the rock. Use the magnifying glass to examine the underside of the small piece of lichen you scraped off the rock. Also examine with the magnifying glass the spot you exposed on the surface of the rock.

Continue to scrape with the small screwdriver the spot you exposed on the surface of the rock. Next, scrape with the screwdriver a spot on the rock that is not covered with a lichen.

Observations

What does the surface of the lichen look like? Is the lichen easy to remove from the surface of the rock? Are the lichens that cover the rock thick or thin?

Can you see tiny particles of rock on the underside of the piece of lichen you removed? Does the spot you exposed on the surface of the rock contain tiny particles of rock?

Does the spot you exposed on the surface of the rock feel crumbly when you scrape it with the small screwdriver? When you scrape a spot on the rock that

is not covered with lichens, does the rock feel hard or crumbly?

Discussion

You should discover that the rock under the lichen is crumbly and contains tiny particles of rock. By comparison, the surface of the rock not covered by lichens should be harder and less crumbly. You may also observe tiny particles of rock on the underside of the piece of lichen you scraped from the rock. These observations show that lichens can break down rock into smaller particles that can become soil.

Lichens are thin patches of plants that can grow on rocks and the bark of trees. Although they appear as one single plant, lichens are actually communities of two separate tiny plants living closely together. The two separate tiny plants that make up lichens are algae and fungi.

The algae and fungi that make up lichens depend on each other for food and protection. Such a relationship is called a symbiotic relationship. In lichens, the symbiotic relationship works this way—the algae produce food by photosynthesis for themselves and the fungi while the fungi protect the algae and provide water and some mineral nutrients to the algae.

Lichens are called pioneer plants because they are some of the first plants to attach and grow on rocks. Lichens play an important role in the formation of soil.

Chemical substances made by the lichens gradually dissolve and break down the rocks to which they cling into tiny particles. The tiny rock particles collect under the lichen and mix with organic material from the lichens and other living things to form soil.

Eventually mosses and other plants start to grow in the soil made by the lichens. These plants make more soil by breaking down the rocks to which they are attached. They also provide organic material for the soil.

One way larger plants break down rocks is with their roots. As these plants work their roots through tiny cracks in the rocks, tiny pieces of the rock are split off and become part of the soil around the plants.

Soil is also made by weathering. Weathering is the natural breakdown of rocks by wind, water, and sunlight. Together, plants and weathering make nearly all the soil on land.

Other Things to Try

Moss is also a pioneer plant. Use a screwdriver to gently pry up a piece of moss from a moss-covered rock. What do you observe?

Look for plants growing in cracks in concrete sidewalks. Are the plants in the cracks breaking up the sidewalk?

Experiment #9

What Effects Does Irrigation Have on Soil?

Materials

A stove   Measuring cup

Water from a sink faucet

A clean, two-quart saucepan

Procedure

ASK AN ADULT TO HELP YOU WITH THIS EXPERI-
MENT. DO NOT USE A STOVE BY YOURSELF.

Add four cups of water (almost one liter) from a sink
faucet to a two-quart saucepan. You can use a larger
saucepan if you do not have one that holds only two
quarts. Heat the water to boiling. Continue to boil until
nearly all the water has boiled away. This may take
thirty minutes or longer. Reduce the heat and allow the
water remaining in the saucepan to slowly evaporate.

Make sure to turn off the stove when all the water
has disappeared. The saucepan will be hot, so let it cool
before you clean it with soap and water.

Observations

After approximately half of the water has boiled away,

does a white film start to form on the side of the saucepan above the surface of the boiling water? When all the water has evaporated from the saucepan, do you see a white film coating the bottom and side of the saucepan?

Discussion

Your results may be slightly different than what is discussed here. Different water supplies may contain different amounts of dissolved salts. If you do not find salts in your water supply, try the first experiment in the section "Other Things to Try."

When the water in the saucepan boils, liquid water is changed into a gas, or vapor. The vapor escapes the saucepan as steam. Heat energy from the stove supplies the energy needed to change the water from a liquid to a vapor.

Heat energy from the stove can only change the water in the saucepan from a liquid to a vapor. Salts dissolved in the water remain in the liquid of the boiling water. As water boils away from the saucepan, the salts in the water become more concentrated. After about half of the water has boiled away, you should start to see a white film form on the inside of the saucepan. This white film is the salts that were dissolved in the water. When all the water is boiled away, you should see a white film on the side and bottom of the saucepan.

All natural waters contain salts dissolved in them. Some natural waters contain more dissolved salts than others. For example, oceans contain more dissolved salts than most rivers and lakes.

Most rainwater contains few dissolved salts. However, as the rainwater flows as runoff on the surface of land, it picks up salts from the land. Also, as rainwater soaks into the ground, it dissolves salts in the soil. These are two main reasons why natural waters, like rivers, lakes, oceans, and groundwater, contain salts dissolved in them.

A major use of water is the irrigation of crops. In the United States, over eighty billion gallons of water are used each day to irrigate crops. Water for irrigation is either groundwater, pumped from wells, or surface water, pumped or diverted from rivers or lakes.

Nearly all the irrigation water not used by the plants evaporates. Very little of the water soaks deep enough into the ground to become part of the groundwater. As the irrigation water evaporates from the soil, the salts that were dissolved in the water are left in the soil. With continued irrigation, excess salts build up in the soil. This process is called salinization.

Most crops do not grow well, and may even die, in soil that contains too many salts. In some areas of the world, salinization of the soil caused by irrigation has severely damaged cropland. The cropland either cannot be used or must be flushed with water to rid it of salt to make the soil fertile again.

Rivers that flow through areas that are heavily irrigated can also become more salty. It has been found that the amount of salt in the Colorado River increases nearly twenty times as the river passes through irrigated cropland of Colorado and Arizona.

One way that has been developed to reduce salinization of the soil during irrigation is with trickle, or drip, irrigation. In trickle irrigation, water is slowly delivered directly to just the roots of plants. Not only does this technique reduce evaporation of water, it also uses less water.

In the future, new techniques, like trickle irrigation, will need to be developed and used to irrigate crops.

Otherwise, valuable cropland may become useless because of salt built up in the soil.

Other Things to Try

Repeat this experiment with natural, noncarbonated, bottled spring water. Many varieties are available in most large grocery stores. Do most of the ones you try contain dissolved salts?

Collect some rainwater the next time it rains. Boil the rainwater to dryness. Are there dissolved salts in your rainwater?

IV. Recycling

When we are through with objects made of metal, plastic, glass, or paper, what do we do with them? Too often, in modern times, the answer has been to just throw them away.

There are more than 5,000 landfills in the United States where trash and garbage are buried. It has been estimated that more than 240 billion pounds of solid wastes (trash and garbage) are taken to these landfills every year. That is about a thousand pounds for every person in the United States.

The space in these landfills is filling up, and it is difficult to find acceptable sites for new landfills. Around the world, more trash and garbage are being generated every day. This trash and garbage can cover the land and prevent its use for other, more attractive purposes.

To use our resources wisely and reduce trash and garbage, we need to learn to reuse, recycle, and reduce. To reuse means to use the same thing more than once. To recycle means to use the same material over and over. To reduce means to get by with less.

In these experiments, you will learn how to recycle household trash, separate plastic objects by a special code, make your own recycled paper, and use the same water more than once.

Experiment #10

How Much of Your Household Trash Can Be Recycled?

Materials

A pen   Tape

Household trash

Six index cards or pieces of paper

Six paper grocery bags or containers to separate recyclable items

Procedure

You will need the permission and maybe the help of an adult in your household to carry out this sorting process of all your household trash.

On each of the six cards write either the word "plastic," "mixed paper," "newspaper," "steel can," "aluminum," or "glass." Tape these cards on the bags or on the containers you will be using to collect and separate your recyclable material.

As the trash in your household is ready to be thrown away, divide it into one of seven categories. If the item to be thrown away is plastic, paper or cardboard, newspaper, steel can, aluminum, or glass, put it in the correct labeled bag. If it is not one of these items, it can be included with your regular household garbage.

Steel cans and tinned steel cans will attract a magnet whereas aluminum will not. Cans that attract a magnet should be placed in the steel can bag. Plastic containers, glass, and steel cans need to be rinsed with water and drained prior to saving.

For this experimental activity, it may be convenient to have one trash can for recyclable material and one trash can for regular garbage. As the can for recyclable materials becomes full, those items can be divided into

the labeled bags or containers. If needed, get additional bags for some categories of recyclable materials. Be sure to crush and flatten any of the material as much as possible so it takes up the least possible space.

Continue this sorting for at least seven days. To compare the amounts of each of the recyclable categories, you will estimate the amount of each type of trash you collected after one week. Use one size bag, such as a grocery-store paper bag, as a comparison. Write down how much of your standard-sized grocery bag was filled with each type of recyclable material.

Observations

How much of a standard-sized grocery bag is filled by the plastic material, the mixed paper, the newspaper, the steel cans, the aluminum, the glass, and the household garbage? Of which material do you have the most?

Discussion

The results of each household will be different and will change from one week to the next. However, here are the results for one week for one household of two adults and four children: The standard-sized grocery bags filled by each type of trash were 2.5 (two and one-half) bags of discarded trash, 0.25 (one-quarter) bag of plastic, 1.5 (one and one-half) bags of mixed paper, 0.3 (three-tenths) bag of newspaper, 0.1 (one-tenth) bag of steel cans, 0.15 (approximately one-sixth) bag of aluminum, and 0.20 (one-fifth) bag of glass.

Note that the total amount of recyclable material was equal to the amount of trash and garbage remaining to be thrown away. In this experiment, even more material could be recycled by saving scraps of food and vegetable matter. Instead of becoming garbage, these food scraps can be added to a compost pile to be changed to a natural fertilizer.

In most places in the United States, the household trash is taken to a landfill and buried. Most households could eliminate from 59 to 90 percent of their discarded trash. You will probably find that the largest amount of recyclable material is mixed paper because of the large number of things we buy that come in cardboard and paper packaging.

The recyclable material you have collected can be divided into smaller groups. For example, the glass can be divided into clear, green, or brown. There are many different types of plastics, and these are indicated by a number on the bottom of the item. Plastics with a number "1" or "2" on the bottom are the ones most commonly recycled. Corrugated containers (large boxes), cardboard such as cereal boxes, and paper may need to be separated out of the mixed paper category.

Recycling has become more important because of the increased cost of disposing household trash in landfills, the need to conserve resources, and the desire to avoid starting new landfills.

Americans throw away hundreds of billions of

pounds of solid waste every year. Most of the time, we use something one time and then get rid of it. It makes more sense to use the same material over and over rather than discarding it and burying it in a landfill. One example is drink containers. Some states require deposits on containers, and as a result, these states recycle as much as 95 percent of beverage containers. Also, some states with deposits on containers have reduced litter along roads by as much as 80 percent.

Recycling aluminum has been highly successful because it saves energy and money. Recycled aluminum saves 95 percent of the energy required to make aluminum from natural ore. In 1991 there were 91 billion aluminum cans made, and 57 billion of these cans were returned to be recycled and made into new aluminum cans.

Other Things to Try

This experimental activity is one you can continue for the rest of your life. You can continue to divide household trash into different categories, but you need to find a place to take the recyclable material. If you do not have curbside pickup of recyclable material where you live, have an adult help you find a place to take items for recycling. Your local government may have a recycling center, or there may be companies that collect or buy material for recycling in your area.

Experiment #11

How Can You Identify Different Types of Plastics for Recycling?

Materials

A variety of plastic containers

Procedure

The Society of Plastics Industry has developed a code to identify and aid in the recycling of plastic containers and bottles. This code uses a number in the center of a triangle and usually a letter code below the triangle. The code is molded into the bottom of most plastic containers.

Look on the bottom of as many different plastic containers as you can find in your household. For each type of container, write down the type of container, such as milk jug, peanut butter jar, or plastic grocery bag. Next to the type of container, write down the number found on the bottom of the container.

Observations

How many different types of plastics did you identify? What number code of plastic was the most common? What kinds of containers were made from each type of plastic?

Discussion

The code numbers, code names, and possible sources of plastic products are listed below:

#	NAME	SOURCES
1	PETE Polyethylene terephthalate	Peanut butter jar, carbonated drink bottle
2	HDPE High-density polyethylene	Milk jug, plastic grocery bag
3	V Vinyl (such as polyvinylchloride)	Vinegar bottle
4	LDPE Low-density polyethylene	Container lid, some plastic grocery bags
5	PP Polypropylene	Squeeze bottle
6	PS Polystyrene	Yogurt container, plastic fast-food containers
7	OTHER	Miscellaneous category for any other types

You probably found some but not all of these types of plastics among items in your household. High-density polyethylene (2, HDPE), may be the one you find most often. It is widely used for milk jugs, water and juice jugs, and detergent bottles. Recycled HDPE can be made into similar containers or into such things as drain pipes, traffic cones, toys, and furniture. Unlike aluminum cans, this plastic is not always used over and over for the same container.

Plastics are made from polymer molecules. Polymer molecules are large molecules made from long chains of smaller molecules connected together. For example, a polystyrene polymer is made of hundreds to thousands of styrene molecule units connected together. Plastic is used to make thousands of different items because plastics are lightweight, strong, and can be easily molded into various shapes.

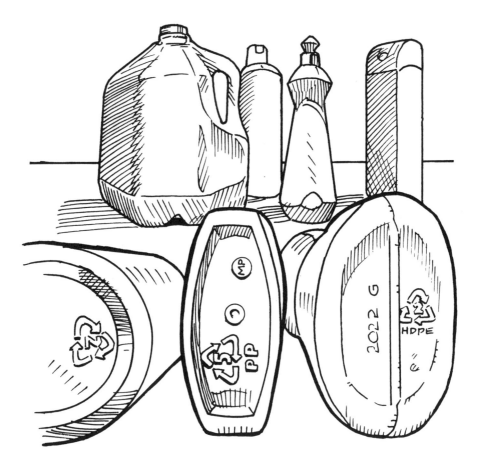

Billions of pounds of plastic are used in the United States every year. The plastics industry wants to increase the amount of recycled plastics. The plastics industry must compete with aluminum, glass, and tinned-steel containers that are recycled in greater numbers at a variety of manufacturing plants.

To increase the amount of plastic recycled in the United States, codes were added to plastic containers so that consumers could sort the plastics for recycling. More than 4,000 communities in the United States collect plastics for recycling. The most common types of plastics collected for recycling are the polyethylene terephthalate (1, PETE or 1, PET) and high-density polyethylene (2, HDPE). In fact, most plastic containers found in grocery stores could be recycled.

Companies as well as individuals are trying to reduce the amount of solid wastes. Some companies are collecting and reusing packaging material used in shipping items. Some of the plastic chips such as polystyrene used in packaging have been replaced with material made from vegetable starch. This biodegradable packaging material will break down naturally in the environment. It will dissolve in water and can be used in compost piles.

Other Things to Try

You can help separate your household plastics for recycling. Use the number code to help identify those items that can be recycled and separate them from the regular trash. Your community may collect plastics for recycling. Ask an adult in your household to help you find a location that collects recycled plastic containers.

In addition to recycling, we could all use fewer things that are made to be used once and then thrown away. Try to think of ways you can reduce your use of disposable (throwaway) items.

Experiment #12

How Do You Make Recycled Paper?

Materials

Newspaper   A measuring cup

A blender or food processor   A tablespoon

A board at least three by six inches in size

Two three- by six-inch pieces of metal screen

(type used in screen doors)

Procedure

HAVE AN ADULT RUN THE BLENDER OR FOOD PROCESSOR. HAVE AN ADULT HELP YOU PREPARE THE PIECES OF METAL SCREEN. Take a full piece of newspaper and tear it into pieces about the size of quarters. Tear enough pieces to fill two cups with pieces of paper. Drop these pieces of newsprint into a food processor or blender. Add two cups of water to the food processor or blender and cover. Have an adult turn on the food processor or blender and run for about a minute or until the paper is turned into a mushy pulp. (See "Other Things to Try" for a different method that does not require a blender or food processor.)

Pour the paper pulp and water mixture into a bowl. Add three tablespoons of cornstarch to a cup of water and stir. Add the cornstarch water to the bowl of paper pulp and stir together to mix well.

Place one piece of metal screen on a piece of newspaper and place some of the paper pulp on the screen. Spread out enough of the pulp to completely cover the screen. Place a second piece of screen wire on top of the paper pulp and a board on top of this screen. Push down on the screen with the board to flatten the paper. Water will be squeezed out of the pulp so you may want to do this outside or in a sink.

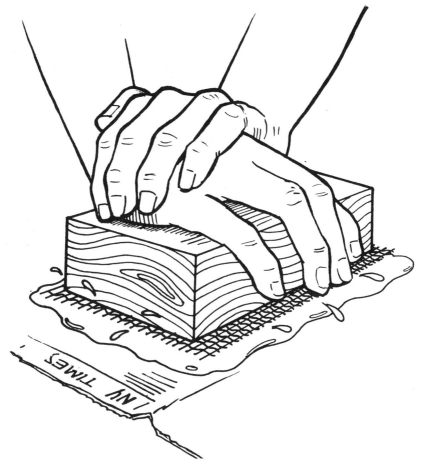

Remove the board and top screen and set the bottom screen and paper aside to dry. The paper will dry overnight or in a few hours if placed in the sunshine on a warm day.

After the paper is dry, gently peel it off the bottom screen. Try writing on the paper with a pen, pencil, and marker.

Observations

What color is your recycled paper? How does the surface feel when you touch it? In what ways is this recycled paper different from notebook paper? Can you write on it with a pencil, pen, and marker?

Discussion

Newsprint, used in making newspapers, is a thin paper made from wood pulp. Pulp is a collection of cellulose fibers used in making paper. In this experimental activity, pieces of newsprint are turned into pulp and then into recycled paper. The process used in industry for making high-quality recycled paper is more complicated than what you did in this experiment, but the basic process is similar.

Your recycled paper should have a gray color because the black ink used in printing is spread throughout the paper. However, you should be able to write on your paper with a pencil, pen, and marker. A dark pen or marker may show up best because of the gray color of your recycled paper. The paper you made will probably be thicker and rougher than paper you normally use for writing.

The ancient Egyptians used papyrus reeds for writing, and the Chinese invented the use of the cellulose fibers taken from plants and trees to make paper. The first paper made in the United States, beginning in 1690, was made of recycled fibers taken from cotton and linen rags.

By the 1930s, almost all the paper made in the United States was made from new wood pulp from freshly cut trees. During World War II, when conservation and recycling were encouraged, about one-third of the paper made in the United States was from recycled material. The amount of recycling decreased after World War II, but has increased in recent years. However, people in the United States are not yet recycling as great a percentage of paper as they did almost fifty years ago.

The United States produces more paper and paperboard products than any other country. Americans use more than 140 billion pounds (64 billion kilograms) of paper each year. That is about 560 pounds for each of the 250 million persons in the United States. It has been estimated that the average office worker in the United States throws away more than 150 pounds of paper each year.

We could be more efficient and use less paper, and we could recycle much more paper than we do now.

This would help reduce the amount of trash that cities and communities must put in landfills or burn. Most, but not all, of the trees used in the manufacture of paper are planted just for this purpose so that as trees are cut, new trees are planted to take their place. In addition to using less trees, making paper products from recycled paper rather than new wood pulp uses about one-third less energy and reduces a great deal of the pollution associated with paper manufacturing.

Other Things to Try

If you want to try making paper without using a blender or food processor, you can use white tissue paper. Tear enough tissue into small pieces to fill a cup. The smaller the pieces the better. Add two cups of water and let the mixture set overnight. Use this pulp to finish making the paper as indicated in the original experiment. This paper will be white since there was no ink on the paper.

Continue the experiment to see how many pieces of recycled paper can be made from one page of newspaper. You can save the pulp to use at a later time to make paper. You can use larger pieces of screen if you want to make bigger pieces of paper.

Experiment with different techniques to see how you can make your paper thinner and smoother. Try adding less or more corn starch to see if this changes the characteristics of the paper.

Experiment #13

Can Recycled Water Be Used To Water Plants?

Materials

A bucket	Soap
Potting soil	Masking tape
A sink	Two cups
Two planting pots	Marker
A package of dry lima beans	

Procedure

Place the bucket in a sink where the water from the faucet will go into the bucket. Turn on the water and wash your hands with soap as you normally would. Then soap your hands and wash them off again. Continue washing your hands until the bucket is about one-half to two-thirds full. You will save the water in this bucket to water growing plants.

Fill two medium-sized (about six inches across) planting pots about three-fourths full of potting soil or other nutrient-rich soil. Place ten lima beans on the surface of the soil in each pot. Cover these lima beans with about an inch of additional soil. Place a piece of masking tape on the first pot and write "graywater" on this piece of tape. Place a piece of masking tape on the second pot and write "pure water" on this piece of tape. Place both pots in a sunny spot where they can stay for at least a week.

After planting the beans, add a cup of water from the bucket to wet the soil in the "graywater" pot. Add a cup of water taken directly from the sink tap to wet the soil in the "pure water" pot. Repeat this procedure of adding water each day as necessary to keep the soil wet. Add the same amount of water to each pot daily but only add the soapy water from the bucket to the pot marked "graywater." Only use tap water from the sink for the "pure water" pot.

Observe the pots each day for at least a week.

Observations

Do you see lima beans begin to grow and break through the soil? Do lima beans begin to grow in each pot? How many of the lima beans are growing in each pot at the end of seven days?

Discussion

The soapy water that you collected in the bucket would normally go down the drain. This used water is sometimes referred to as graywater. It is called graywater because it is not pure since it contains soap. However, graywater is not contaminated like water from a toilet.

In your experiment, you should find that the lima

beans grow in both pots. The plants grow with either pure water or graywater. Not all the lima beans will grow because some seeds may not germinate or begin to grow. After seven days, you will probably have about five or six growing plants. The faster-growing plants may be about four or five inches tall. Some of the plants grow faster than others. You should find that the graywater works as well as pure water for watering plants. Since soapy water is basic, the graywater may work best on plants that prefer alkaline soil.

Graywater comes from activities such as taking

showers, taking baths, shaving, and washing hands. Some things like kitchen grease should not be allowed into graywater. However, graywater makes up more than half the water used in most homes.

In some places, graywater is collected in a tank, and the water is used to water gardens. This is especially useful in dry areas where there may be a shortage of water. By using graywater, the same water can be recycled because it is used twice—first for washing and second for watering plants. This reduces the total amount of water used and can reduce the amount of water that must be treated by sewage treatment plants.

There are many other ways to reduce the amount of water we use in our homes. Trying some of these methods can save many thousands of gallons of water each year in a single household. See if an adult in your household would try some of the methods discussed below.

Low-flow faucet aerators can be placed on all the kitchen and bathroom faucets to save water. A low-flow faucet aerator mixes air with water and can make the water flow seem greater even though it uses only half as much water. These simple devices are different than the usual screens normally found on the bottom of faucets and can save water.

Devices can be added to reduce the water in the tank on the back of a toilet. Each flush of a regular toilet may use five to seven gallons of water. Toilets can flush as well with less water each time. A clean plastic bottle filled with water and weighted down with some stones can be placed in the toilet tank. You just have to make sure the size and placement of the bottle do not interfere with the toilet flushing mechanism.

Low-flow shower heads can replace regular shower heads. Showers may use water at a rate of five to seven gallons a minute. A ten-minute shower could use seventy gallons of water. Low-flow shower heads can reduce water used to about three gallons per minute and also save energy because less water must be heated.

Other Things to Try

Continue this experiment by watering the plants daily to see how much more the lima bean plants will grow. You may need to move the plants to a larger pot or into the ground as they begin to need more space for roots.

Repeat the original experiment with a stronger soap solution. Add one-half cup of liquid hand soap to a bucket of water. Use this water for your graywater. Does having this extra soap in the water affect the plant growth?

V. Handling Wastes

Have you ever thought about how much garbage you generate? According to estimates from the United States Environmental Protection Agency, the average person in the United States produces almost four pounds of solid waste (garbage and trash) each day. Presently, nearly 180 million tons of solid waste is generated in the United States each year. This amount is expected to rise as our population continues to increase.

Most of the solid waste generated today is buried under dirt in sanitary landfills. This method of solid waste disposal was once cheap. It is becoming more expensive because many landfills are nearly full and land for new landfills is difficult to find. In addition, regulations require that new landfills must be carefully built to avoid polluting surrounding groundwater and air.

Although convenient for those of us who produce garbage, burying garbage in landfills is wasteful. It is wasteful because nearly all of household garbage could be recycled.

About 25 percent of our garbage is made up of metal, glass, and plastic containers that can be reused or recycled into other useful products. Food waste and yard waste also account for nearly 25 percent of the material in our garbage. Most of this food and yard waste can be recycled by composting, which produces valuable nutrients for plants. Or it could be changed into a fuel. The major material (39 percent) in our garbage is paper and paper products, which can also be recycled.

We, the producers of garbage, are part of the waste disposal problem. We, the producers of garbage, must also be part of the solution. In the experiments that follow you will learn more about how we do and can handle waste.

Experiment #14

What Happens to Freshly Cut Grass When It Is Piled Together?

Materials

Freshly cut grass clippings   A rake
A cooking thermometer   Water
Piece of paper   Pencil or pen

Procedure

Ask an adult to help you collect freshly cut grass clippings. Try to gather an amount that would fill at least a large grocery bag.

In a shady area of a yard, pile the freshly cut grass clippings into a mound. Read the temperature on the cooking thermometer and write this temperature on the paper. Label this temperature "start temperature." Now, completely insert the thermometer into the mound of grass. Briefly remove the thermometer after each hour for three hours and read the temperature. Make sure to insert the thermometer back into the mound of grass after each temperature reading. Record your temperatures on a piece of paper. Label your temperatures "hour 1," "hour 2," and "hour 3."

Leave the thermometer in the mound of grass

clippings overnight. Remove the thermometer the next day and record its temperature. Label this temperature "overnight."

After you are through with the thermometer, ask an adult to wash the cooking thermometer thoroughly with soap and water. The thermometer should be placed in boiling water for five minutes before being used in cooking again. DO NOT USE THE STOVE BY YOURSELF.

Use a rake to spread out the grass clippings. What do you observe? Place your hand above the grass clippings. What do you feel? If the grass clippings appear dry, sprinkle some water on them. Rake the grass clippings back into a mound. Each day for a week, spread out the grass clippings, sprinkle some water on them if they appear dry, and then rake them back into a mound.

Observations

Does the temperature inside the mound of grass clippings become greater than the surrounding air temperature? What is the temperature inside the grass mound after one hour? What is the temperature after three hours?

Can you feel the heat coming from the mound of grass clippings? Do you see steam rising from the mound of grass clippings? What does the mound of grass clippings smell like after several hours?

What is the temperature inside the mound of grass clippings the next morning? Do you see steam rising from the grass clippings when you spread the clippings with a rake? What color are the grass clippings?

Does the size of the mound of grass clippings appear to get smaller after several days? What do the grass clippings look like after a week?

Discussion

You should find that changes start to take place in the mound of grass clippings soon after you build the mound. You should notice that the temperature inside the mound of grass clippings rises and becomes greater than the temperature of the surrounding air. You may even record a temperature as high as 71° C (160° F).

If the air is cool, you may see water vapor rising as clouds from the top of the mound. These clouds also tell you that the mound of grass clippings is hot. In addition to the steam rising from the mound, you may smell a sweet, earthy odor coming from the mound of grass clippings.

These changes in the mound of grass clippings are due to the breakdown or decomposition of the grass clippings. This decomposition is caused by microorganisms on the blades of grass and in the soil that was collected with the grass clippings. These soil organisms include various bacteria, fungi, and algae.

The grass clippings serve as food for the soil organisms. By decomposing the grass clippings, the soil organisms obtain energy to live, grow, and multiply. In the process, the soil organisms change chemical substances in the grass clippings into important nutrients. These nutrients enter the soil and are used by living plants and soil animals.

Soil organisms such as bacteria and fungi are called decomposers. Decomposers are nature's way of recycling dead animal matter by breaking down complex chemical substances in dead plant and animal matter into simple chemical substances. These simpler chemical substances then become nutrients for living plants and soil animals.

Decomposers are called the ultimate recyclers. Without decomposers, chemical substances needed by living plants and animals would not be recycled. If chemical substances needed for life were not recycled, then life would disappear from the earth.

After about a week you may see earthworms and other small animals, such as beetles, in the decomposed grass clippings. Earthworms and other burrowing animals are called secondary decomposers. They usually start to appear in decaying matter after bacteria and fungi have broken down much of the dead plant or animal matter. These secondary decomposers continue the decomposition of the organic matter. In the process, they also mix the newly formed nutrients from the decaying matter with the soil. Earthworms and other burrowing animals also improve the soil with their burrows and holes in the soil. These burrows and holes allow water and air to enter the soil.

Did you know that much of the household garbage that ends up in landfills consists of organic matter from fruits and vegetables that can be recycled into soil nutrients? And nearly 20 percent of the material being buried in landfills is yard waste such as leaves and grass clippings that can be recycled into soil nutrients.

Other Things to Try

Organic matter in household waste and yard waste can be recycled by composting. Composting involves building a pile outdoors with alternate layers of plant material and soil. Over a period of time, bacteria and fungi in the soil decompose the organic waste into a crumbly brown material called humus. Humus is rich in plant nutrients and makes an excellent natural fertilizer.

If you have the space outdoors, ask an adult in your household to help you build a compost pile to recycle food and yard waste from your household. Make sure to ask an adult to help select a spot in the yard for the compost pile.

You can add just about any plant material to your compost pile. From the yard, you can add leaves, grass clippings, and dead plants. Materials from the kitchen that you can add include vegetable and fruit peels and trimmings, coffee grounds, and even eggshells. You should not add meat scraps to your compost pile because they may attract animals. Also, decomposing meat scraps produce a foul odor. Also avoid adding cooked vegetables and fruits to your compost pile because they may also make a foul odor.

Occasionally you will need to add water to your compost pile to keep it moist, and about once a week ask an adult to help you turn your compost pile with a shovel or forked garden tool. To turn your compost pile, you want to try to mix the material in your pile so that the material that was on the bottom of the pile is now on the top and the material that was on the top is now on the bottom. When your compost becomes brown and crumbly, you are ready to use it as a natural fertilizer. This may take several weeks.

Remember, composting not only makes an excellent natural fertilizer, it also saves valuable landfill space.

Experiment #15

Can You Compare the Decomposition of Different Materials?

Materials

A piece of aluminum foil	A piece of styrofoam
A page of newspaper	A knife
A measuring cup	A planting pot
A tomato	A banana
Soil	A trowel or small shovel
Water	Scissors

A piece of plastic such as from a six-pack cover

Procedure

ASK AN ADULT TO HELP YOU WITH THIS EXPERI-MENT. Have an adult use a knife to cut a piece of tomato and a piece of banana each about the size of a quarter. Use a pair of scissors to cut out pieces of aluminum, styrofoam, newspaper, and plastic about the size of quarters.

Use a trowel or small shovel to dig up dark soil and fill a planting pot about three-fourths full of this soil. Lay the six objects: tomato, banana, aluminum, styrofoam, newspaper, and plastic on the soil in a circle around the inside of the pot. Now cover the six objects with a layer of soil about an inch thick. Pour one cup of water on the soil and set the pot inside in a warm spot or outside if the weather is warm.

Wait one week and then remove the top layer of soil. Dig up the six objects. Place what you find on a page of newspaper.

Observations

Do you find all six objects? After you brush off the soil, do the objects look the same? Can you describe any differences in the objects before they were buried and after one week of being buried?

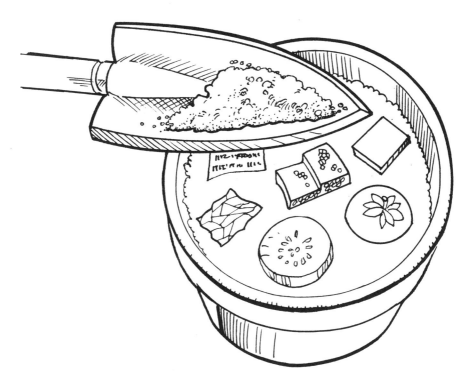

Discussion

You probably found that the aluminum, styrofoam, and plastic were not changed by being in the soil for one week. The piece of newspaper may have yellowed slightly but otherwise is probably not different. However, the tomato and banana may be much different. You may have trouble finding the tomato and banana. If you do find them, they may be much smaller, be black, and be falling apart.

Decomposition is the process in which some matter breaks down into simpler parts. Decomposition can be caused by light, heat, chemical reactions, or the action of bacteria and other microorganisms. The tomato and banana are living material and are decomposed by bacteria present in the soil. Given enough time in the presence of soil microorganisms, the tomato and banana will completely decompose or break down into simpler molecules. The original banana and tomato will eventually be gone. However, the aluminum, plastic, and styrofoam are not broken down by soil bacteria. Paper mostly is made of fibers of cellulose, which comes from wood and so can be broken down by nature but may require much longer than food matter.

Soil comes from living and nonliving matter. Nonliving matter in soil includes the air, water, and particles of clay, silt, and sand. Soil also includes organic matter that comes from dead plants and animals and the tiny microscopic organisms that live on this decaying material. Even a teaspoon of soil may contain billions of bacteria, protozoa, and other microorganisms.

Bacteria, protozoa, and fungi (such as molds and mushrooms) can feed on waste products from live animals, dead plants, or dead animals. Warm temperatures and moisture help bacteria grow and multiply. Extreme heat or cold can kill microorganisms, which is why we refrigerate food and cook food that might spoil such as meat. Some types of bacteria can cause disease in humans, and so we try to prevent these from growing.

The type of bacteria that feed on matter that comes from living things helps recycle carbon, nitrogen, and other elements on which living things depend. Decay and decomposition allow essential elements and molecules to be used by other living things. Without decay, all the matter would be locked in a living organism when it died, unavailable for the growth of other living things. For example, minerals and nutrients mix with water to form a soil solution. Plants absorb these needed minerals and nutrients along with water from this soil solution.

Since bacteria can not decompose metal, styrofoam, and plastic, these materials only slowly decompose by chemical means in the environment. For example, it has been estimated that the time it takes litter above ground to decay is tin can—100 years, aluminum can—200 to 500 years, plastic (from six-pack cover)—450 years, and styrofoam—more than 500 years.

Just because a garbage truck comes to the street where we live and hauls away our trash, it does not disappear. Much of the trash is taken to landfills where the trash is dumped in a pit and then covered over with dirt. The trash may be covered, but it is not gone. Many cities are filling up their landfills and need to find space for increasing amounts of trash. We can help reduce the amount of trash that must be placed in landfills by conservation (using less) and recycling (using over). For example, the aluminum foil from an aluminum can does not need to be buried but can be used to make new aluminum cans. Every aluminum can you recycle saves energy and reduces trash.

Other Things to Try

Try repeating this experiment with different types of material and determine which things decompose the fastest. Try burying some things in the ground and then digging them up a month later to see how much they have changed.

Try putting some pieces of vegetable matter (carrots, potatoes, lettuce, or grapes) in the soil and some scraps of the same vegetables in a plastic bag in a refrigerator and compare how fast each decays.

Try putting some scraps of vegetable matter or meat near an ant colony and watch how the ants use this food source.

Experiment #16

Can Plant Material Be Changed Into a Fuel?

Materials

Water

A jar with lid

Several large, dead, dried leaves

Rid-X (available in the cleaning section of most grocery stores and also in hardware stores)

Procedure

Crumble up several large, dead, dried leaves. Place the crumbled leaves in a jar. Ask an adult to add one tablespoon of Rid-X to the jar. Completely fill the jar with water. Place the uncovered jar outside in a warm spot.

Once each day for two weeks look at the crumbled leaves in the jar. Put the lid on the jar, gently shake the jar, and make your observations. Remove the lid. Add water to the jar if the water level in the jar drops.

Smell the gases produced in the jar after a week. To do this, shake the jar and then gently wave one of your hands over the top of the jar to move the smell to your nose.

When you have finished the experiment, pour the contents of the jar on the ground. Rinse the jar several times with water.

Observations

After a couple of days do you see bubbles on the crumbled leaves? Do the bubbles rise to the surface of the water when you gently shake the jar?

Do the leaves turn black in about a week? Do bubbles still form when the leaves turn black?

Does a film form on the surface of the water after about a week? How would you describe the smell of the gases produced in the jar?

Discussion

Rid-X is a nontoxic product used to keep septic systems working properly. Septic systems are tanks used in

some places instead of sewer systems to treat household waste water. Rid-X contains various bacteria from natural sources. These bacteria break down organic material from plants and animals. In underground septic tanks, these bacteria break down solid organic waste into a liquid that then flows into the ground. In this experiment, you are using Rid-X to break down the organic material in dead leaves.

After several days, you should start to see the formation of bubbles in the jar. These bubbles are due to gases made by the breakdown of the dead leaves. This breakdown of the leaves is being done by bacteria from the Rid-X.

In this jar, there is no air around the leaves. The bacteria can break down the leaves without using air. This is called anaerobic decomposition. When bacteria use air to break down organic material, the process is called aerobic decomposition.

One of the major gases made by bacteria during anaerobic decomposition is methane. The gas bubbles you see in this experiment contain methane.

Methane is a simple organic molecule. Each methane molecule consists of one carbon atom to which four hydrogen atoms are attached. Methane is sometimes called marsh gas because it is the gas produced in marshes and swamps. Methane is made in marshes and swamps by the anaerobic decomposition of dead plant material.

Methane is a flammable gas. It is the chief component

in natural gas, which is an important fuel. Of the fossil fuels, like oil and coal, methane is the cleanest-burning fuel. When methane burns, only water and carbon dioxide are formed.

Like coal and petroleum, natural gas is not a renewable energy source. However, methane gas made by anaerobic decomposition of organic material by bacteria is a renewable energy source. A renewable energy source is one that can be replaced and produced again.

A rich source of organic material is city sewage. Although not common yet, some communities in the United States have waste treatment plants that include special tanks called methane digesters. In a methane digester, municipal sewage is decomposed by bacteria into methane that is collected and used as a fuel.

Methane digesters can also be used to convert animal manure into methane. Feedlots, which are places where large numbers of cattle and pigs are kept and fed, generate large quantities of animal manure. At some of these feedlots, digesters are used to convert animal waste into methane. In the future, more feedlots will convert their animal waste into fuel because it will generate energy and decrease the amount of pollution entering our environment.

In some countries, methane digesters are common and are used to make methane fuel from plant and animal waste. For example, in China, it is estimated that over half a million small methane digesters operate in homes and farms to generate methane fuel.

Methane gas is also generated in sanitary landfills. Sanitary landfills are areas where many communities dispose and bury their garbage. Much of this buried garbage is made of organic material that bacteria in the soil can decompose into methane gas. Some communities have sealed their landfills in order to trap the methane generated from the decomposing garbage in the landfill. The collected methane is then used as a fuel. Most new landfills are being built so they can capture the methane generated in the decomposing garbage for use as a fuel.

In the future, as the world's energy needs increase and as the world's source of nonrenewable sources of energy decrease, the conversion of organic material into methane is likely to become more important.

Other Things to Try

Repeat this experiment with other plant material like grass clippings. Do you get similar results?

Repeat this experiment but do not add Rid-X to the jar of water containing the crumbled leaves. Do you still see the formation of gas bubbles after a couple of days?

Complete List of Materials Used in These Experiments

B
bags, paper
balloon
banana
blender
board, 3" x 6"
bowl, large
bucket

C
clay, artist or
    modeling
coffee filters
containers, plastic
cornstarch
cups, measuring
cups, paper
cups, plastic

F
foil, aluminum

G
grass clippings
grass, patch of
    growing
grassy area

I
index cards

J
jar, large with lid
jars, small

K
knife

L
leaves, large,
    dried
lima beans,
    dry

M
magnifying glass
marker,
    permanent

N
newspaper

P
pan
paper
pen, felt
pencil
pickling lime
pie pans, alumi-
    num
plastic
pots, planting

R
rake
red cabbage
    leaves
Rid-X
rock with lichens

ruler

S
sand
saucepan,
    two-quart
scissors
screens, metal,
    3" x 6"
screwdriver
shovel
sink
soap
soil
soil, potting
spoons,
    measuring
stove
styrofoam

T
tape
thermometer,
    cooking
tomato
trash, household
trowel

V
vinegar

W
water

Index